My World, My Words:

Confessions of a Cluttered Mind

Jacob Grovey

Copyright © 2009 by Jacob Grovey

All rights reserved.

This book or any portion thereof may not be reproduced or used in any manner whatsoever without the express written permission of the publisher except for the use of brief quotations in a book review.

Second edition printed by Global Genius Society, 2022

GlobalGeniusSociety.com

ISBN: 978-1-7363216-3-8

This book is dedicated to the memory of my grandparents, Lillian Moore Jacobs and William Jacobs. Your lives and words have always inspired me to move forward, in spite of the obstacles that are in my way. I pray you are proud of my progress.

1 John 1:4

And we are writing these things so that our joy may be complete.

Table of Contents

To Big Mama…………………………………………..	1
Conversation With God………………………………..	2
The Politics…………………………………….	7
To Dream……………………………………..	9
Suicidal Circle………………………………….	10
Life & Loves…………………………………..	13
Memory of the Cool……………………………..	15
The Blank Canvas Transformation……………………	17
I've Got a Weapon………………………………..	19
Love's Journey…………………………………	20
The Pressure…………………………………..	23
Hope in a Bottle………………………………..	24
Alphabetic Perfection……………………………	26
The Future……………………………………..	28
Mathematics…………………………………..	30
Road to Redemption…………………………….	31

Remember…………………………………………..	42
Be…………………………………………………….	43
Only in America…………………………………..	44
I'm More Interested………………………………	45
Job Description……………………………………..	47
Easily Ignored……………………………………..	49
Acting In Confidence…………………………..	51
My Block……………………………………………	52
Weary………………………………………………...	53
Misconceptions…………………………………..	55
After Elza…………………………………………..	56
(Untitled)……………………………………………	57
Life's Tribulations……………………………..	58
To Dad……………………………………………...	59
Black………………………………………………...	60
My Perspective……………………………………	62
The Story of Beauty…………………………….	64

Get By………………………………………………..	74
Letter to the Lord……………………………………	76
(Untitled)…………………………………………….	78
I Am………………………………………………...	79
Open Letter to Ms. Lady…………………………….	81
Tetris………………………………………………...	83
'09 Revolution………………………………………	84
Love's a Trip………………………………………..	86
New Noose…………………………………………..	88
God is the DJ……………………………………….	89
The Store……………………………………………	91
To Mom……………………………………………..	93
My Life's Symphony………………………………..	94
New Era……………………………………………..	97
My Reality…………………………………………..	99
Let Love Lie…………………………………………	100

Alien Nation……………………………………….	102
Photographic Memory……………………………..	103
My Walkman………………………………………..	105
(Untitled)……………………………………………	107
Another Girl Lost…………………………………	108
Waiting…………………………………………….	109
?...	111
(Untitled)…………………………………………..	113
In Remembrance of Grandpa……………………..	115
The One……………………………………………..	116
My World, My Words…………………………….	117
Thank You………………………………………….	120

Allow me to re-introduce myself....

Hello, my name is Jacob Grovey. When this collection of poetry was originally released, it was done so as I was forced to deal with the apprehension and anxiety that had started to get too comfortable inside of me. I felt I had something to say, so I moved beyond my own fears to set my words free. Now, over a decade later, I feel it is time for those words to be released again.

Although much time has passed since you were first introduced to my work, I still want you to know how much I appreciate you for giving my words a chance to live (or to be alive again). As you dive into this collection of poetry, you will see the title holds true. This, by no means is an organized, categorized book of poetry. After all, you can't really expect organization from a cluttered mind.

Some of the poems will be extensive, while others will be brief. Some of my work will rhyme, while rhyming doesn't properly convey the message of others. Most of the poetry has titles I found to be befitting, but even after all of these years, there are still some that remain untitled. One moment, my words will make it seem like I am in love with the world, but as soon as you turn the page, the abundance of love has seemingly disappeared. Everybody goes through a wide range of emotions, and I am certainly no exception.

I also want it to be known I have written this book disregarding many of the rules of correct punctuation and proper grammar. I know many will frown at that, but context and conversation can often times supersede correctness. Even with that being said, I hope this book is something people of all ages will be able to get something from.

I know it's unrealistic to think everyone will like all of the poems in this book, so that's not my goal. Instead, my objective is to show those who read this book they are not alone in their feelings. I want everyone to get the joy they deserve, but I also want us all to know it's okay to deal with sadness and anger when life isn't going the way we think it should. This book was being processed in my mind for a long time, so I pray you feel it was worth the wait.

To Big Mama

I'm sitting here writing, trying not to cry
And I'm wondering out of everybody, why you had to die
Now it's been many years you've been deceased
You're at home in heaven, so I know you're resting in peace
The memories of your life help me go on
I just talk to you as I look up, instead of the phone
I know you're watching your family from up above
And I'm blessed to have met you and experience your love
There's no more running around, so you can finally rest
No more struggling, no more working….so why am I upset?
I guess when it comes to death, family can be very selfish
We wanted to keep you with us, we just couldn't help it
As I continue to wipe the tears from my face
I also have to smile because I was fortunate to meet a person so great
I appreciate your love and everything you did
You treated everyone the same, which was truly appreciated by all of your grandkids
You were quick to do for others before you did for yourself
And I'm sorry that I just kept begging, instead of trying to help
I'll end this by saying as long as your spirit is around, our family is never alone
And I know I'll see you again when God calls *me* home

Conversation with God

Hearing the voice of God can have a person shook
Especially if he asks if you've taken the time to read His book
He told me He wrote it down so I could take a look
Stealing away from the conversation made me feel like a crook
God stated He needed to ask me a question
"Since when have you been afraid to learn a few lessons?
I'm not trying to change you, that's now what I'm requesting.
I just want you to live a life long enough for you to count your blessings."
Then, He said, "We're both writers, that's a common trait we share. I'll read your stories if you read mine, unless you just don't care."
"That ain't fair," I said."You know that's not true."
"But why don't you show the amount of love to me that I show for you?"
"God, everyday I try my best to live decently?"
"But how do you expect to be at peace with me if you haven't visited with me recently?"
Then He continued, "How many prayers do you send?
Or do you lust for sinful things as if the devil was your friend?
Do you think your grandmother approves of some of the things you do? If she was asked about Jacob, would she be proud of you?"
Dang! Tears began to stream down my face
I had to actually question if I was my family's source of disgrace
In my mouth, the conversation was leaving a bitter taste

I couldn't even remember why it began in the first place

He continued, " You know rap verses, but you know none from the Bible.

Me or Jay-Z, who do you believe is more reliable?

He was the president of Def Jam, but I can bring death to man."

Prior words were comprehensible, but right then, I could truly understand

The plan was for me to get situated on the right road

Where I could believe there was never too heavy a load

At least, not for me to carry

To the truth I had to be married

And never conceive the idea of a divorce

The road would get bumpy, but I had to steer the course

God was silent, so I assumed it was my turn to speak

"God, what if I don't believe in all those who preach?"

"Don't you see? You don't have to believe them to believe in me?

You see, even the preachers are still just some of my kids.

They may make mistakes, but it's to me they are building a bridge

Big enough for everyone in the world to cross

But it's there especially for those who get lost."

He continued, "Take you for example,

There have been plenty of times you been in situations you thought you couldn't handle."

I screamed, "Yeah, those were the times you turned your back!"

"'Not at all. In fact, those were the times when faith, you lacked."

"To be honest God, I was giving up on you."

"But even then, I gave you the strength to pull through."

I smiled, "God, I guess I need to thank you for that."

"Even when you don't think so, Jacob I got your back."

I never would've thought I would hear those words

And although it was unexpected, I'm glad it occurred

"Jacob, I need for you to look back on your life.

Honestly, do you think you have always lived right?"

"Well, to tell the truth, I know I've made mistakes,

But it's very hard work just *trying* to be great."

God said, "Oh, I know, just look at my work.

If I have a bad day, billions of people would get hurt."

"I feel ya," I said. He told me He figured I would

It was also stated I mostly did what I thought was good

"See, I like you kid, that's why I'm so patient.

And when you need help, I'm at my house waiting.

I also understand when you get mad at me,

But understand, I get upset when people commit blasphemy."

"If I've ever done that, I regret my actions."

"A heartfelt apology, now that gives me satisfaction.

You know, out of all of the names in the world, your parents named you Jacob.

That's a biblical name and sometimes I just think you need to believe in me and wake up.

Quit thinking things are always so bad.

You have been blessed with a good life, along with a loving mom and dad.

Not only that, there are friends and family who surround you with love

To top it off, you have a grandmother that's now an angel watching you from above."

Everything he said was 100% true

Then God told a joke, "See, Jamie ain't the only one to make it do what it do."

"God, may I say something I don't know if I've expressed?"

"Of course you may, if you feel you won't have any regrets."

"I was just thinking about my favorite color being blue,

it's probably my favorite because it's what I see when I look up to you."

I could sense He now had a smile

And when it came to me, that probably hadn't happened in a while

"I want you to realize something Jacob, I am your father.

You can call on me 24 hours a day and it's never a bother."

Then His voice faded, I guess it was time to depart

But I knew I could talk again when I spoke from my heart

"God, I know you are more than a heavenly father, but also my friend.

In your son's name I do pray, amen!"

I opened my eyes not knowing if the conversation was real

But I did know every single word that was said was something I could feel

If the discussion was a prayer, I didn't realize

My emotions were overflowing and I still had tears in my eyes

For another discussion, I had nothing but anticipation

I guess that's how it is when God is part of the conversation

The Politics

I can't be politically correct when I'm politically upset
And the thing is, we probably haven't seen the worst of it yet
And now, Bush is the leader of one of the word's most powerful nations
Some said he was gonna do good, well, we've been patiently waiting
Now I've heard Bush don't like black people
And it seems his way into office had to be illegal
I doubt any regal actions will be associated with his name
I guess it runs in the family because for his father you can say the same
Now, I won't let no man made from God harm me
But "dub" must work with the devil the way he's getting rid of the army
Their time @ home is short, but the away trips seem to come back-to-back
Off with dreams and backpacks while spending years in Iraq
We supposedly went over there to find weapons of mass destruction and to aid with justice
Not only have we not found the weapons, but we've continued to give them a reason to not trust us
Some have also said we're making sure their freedom won't be lost
In reality, it's just a case of "dub" trying to show he's the boss
But we can't worry about the people, we can only worry about the political party
We can't see we've done people wrong and simply say, "I'm sorry."

No, some things can't be done because they require too much logic and acknowledgment

Let's continue to disregard the people and just worry about the politics

To Dream

It has been said if you die in a dream, you die in real life

I say, if you won't allow your dreams to live, you are already dead

Suicidal Circle

I heard a conversation between a knife and a wrist
It said certain people should cease to exist
Said the shotgun to the bullet and the bullet to the head
"I agree, some people are better off dead."
Upset when we met, this girl's name was Contessa
At 16 years old, I could tell things were messed up
She said, "I'm fed up with everything in my life.
I'm always too stressed to even sleep at night."
It was more than evident she just needed a friend
"I just really wish my life would end."
"Look, you're a beautiful girl, you have reasons to live."
Her face seemed shocked my words were positive.
"You don't even know me, so I don't know why you have to lie."
She sat down as she quickly began to cry.
Over time I learned why she had been feeling bad lately
She was broke, alone, and now pregnant with a baby
I said, "Maybe this is good, it's like starting anew."
"I'm young, but I ain't dumb. Who are you trying to fool?"
"I'm not fooling anybody because I'm telling the truth.
Life can be beautiful and you can be proof"
Now go back a little while, to some time in the 90s
Fashion is bright colors teamed with a pair of plain Nikes

I'm really young, dressed in a pair of Levis
When I saw a woman with a big belly pass me by
"How old is he?" She asked. My parents replied "Nine."
"Yeah, I'm just a few months away from having mine."
The lady with the stomach stopped and smiled
So her and my parents conversed for a little while
"The thought of the baby keeps me thrivin' inside, but I just lost my job, so I don't know how we'll survive."
My mom grasped her hand tightly and then her face wasn't the same
I didn't know what was going on, but things had just changed
Time passed and I started seeing the lady on a regular basis
Out of all the places she knew, our home seemed like the safest
But when her stomach got larger, we started seeing her less
I guess one of us must have said something to make her upset
With more time, my young mind forgot about the stranger
I forgot about her visits and whatever caused all of her anger
My parents, on the other hand, were a completely different story
The lady stayed on their minds as if they were trying to remember for me
Whatever they were thinking, they normally kept it to themselves
I guess they figured there was nothing I could do to actually help
Then, everything changed that one faithful day
When my folks picked up the paper and seemed blown away
It talked about how a lady who was seven months pregnant had been shot in the head

They were able to save the baby, but the mother was dead
Contessa was the name tattooed to the baby's soul
She was born into a world, that to her, seemed cold
She came into the world alone and she grew up the same
Though she tried to live right, negativity remained
The lady that we met, was the same one who was killed
The Contessa I met was her daughter, (still)
Young she was just two times the age of eight
Her mom committed suicide and the daughter had the same fate.
I heard a conversation between a knife and a wrist
They said certain people should cease to exist
Said the shotgun to the bullet and the bullet to the head
"I agree, some people are better off dead."
The weapons were wrong, but these are the words many are being fed
We'd rather end our troubles than get help instead
Whatever issues we are dealing with, we can't keep them inside
We have to help each other break the vicious circle of suicide

Life & Loves

It seems like with every passing day, I'm in a circle of wrong doings
I'm in love with my writing, but it seems new loves, I keep pursuing
Art, yeah, she was around a long time ago
But it seems, as I grew older, she hardly wanted to show
Back in the day we'd talk daily
No pun intended, but now she acts shady
I guess she's seen me out with some of my other girls
She feels if she ain't #1, she'd rather not be in my world
I don't blame her because I wouldn't want to be #2
And as much as I love her, I just don't know what to do
The crazy thing is, I know it ain't fair
Now I love hip-hop and she thinks I don't care
But I just recently met her and we're just friends
But both writing and art want to make our relationship end
"She's too gangster, narcissistic and too hood"
They don't even know her, how can they say she's no good
Yeah she likes jewelry and spends a lot of time in clubs
But she's passionate about her opinions and that's something I love
Although we're just cool, she gets mad at me for playing trumpet on the side
At times she claims not to care, but she can't hold the truth inside
I told her I knew trumpet way before we met

Even with that, she remains upset

"I've known trumpet since I was ten."

But she says, "I don't want to argue with you again."

I explained that she's doing her own thing, but I still care

She said, "No, you still love her, so don't go there!"

She may be right, but it's something I can't admit

We've been separated many times, but she's someone I can't fully quit

When my girls see each other, lightly put, it's a Jerry Springer situation

But I can't let go because I have prior obligations

Just because I won't quit them, doesn't mean they won't quit me

And living without any of them is something I don't want to see

I've tried to make a decision for years, but I guess it's just not my call

And if I lose them, I'll be glad I lost love, rather than never loved at all

Memory of the Cool

My father called him little brother, my cousins called him Dad
I called him one of the coolest uncles I ever had
When I saw him and my father together, it was almost like something I'd see on tv
My uncle was like a future version of my little brother, and looking at my dad was like seeing me
I think the last time I saw him healthy was back in the summer of '96
During our family reunion, before he really got sick
After that, I heard he was having health issues, but I knew Uncle Maurice was strong
I thought it was something he would overcome, something that wouldn't last too long
I guess it was because of that, we tried not to bring it up
And if someone ever did, I just wanted them to hush
There was no way he wasn't going to be around
When it came to swagger, him and my dad were always battling for the crown
I guess cool is sometimes used as a tool to make fools of those who are around
I know I didn't think about it, but I wonder if even he knew he would soon be heaven bound
He left behind his parents, siblings, and kids of his own

I still wish I could look at my caller ID and see it was him on the phone
But I can't, and that's not fiction, it's simply a fact
He's in heaven with Big Mama, Grandpa and Elza, and we can't get him back
It's still strange to think, a year and a day after losing my grandmother, I lost him too
But we can never forget my uncle, this in memory of the cool

The Blank Canvas Transformation

I started off as a blank canvas that God provided
To my parents to paint a better picture than their parents and that's what go them excited
I'm more than delighted to handle the torch, the fire, and the flame
And though I'm a small in stature, I'm more than big enough to carry on my family's name
You can blame them for my confidence, but me for arrogance
Mama once said I was special and I've acted accordingly ever since
Now, I want to be as fly and free as the birds in the skies and trees
And be as inspirational as the people and things that inspired me
My nest's eggs branch from the roots of my existence
In my world, I show resistance to those not being persistent
Now listen, I want to be the one to burst the bubble
Of any person, place, or thing looking to bring the ones closest to me back to the struggle
And when I go to sleep, I seem to dream of a better place
While trying to focus hard enough to see God's face
And when I pray, I thank the Lord for the new hours I hope to receive
I thank him for putting goals in my head that I continuously try to achieve
And even when I fail, I know I can still succeed
But most of all, I thank him for placing enough love in my heart to love all those who love me

I try to live out my dreams on a daily basis

Be the one to exceed expectations as if I were "The One," like in The Matrix

The safest route has me so sick like Ne-Yo, but it's not of love songs, it's of "thug" songs

The lack of lyricism from liars only seem to prolong

The bad times with bad rhymes

Which constantly bring me to mad times

But I digress, or @ least I try not to stress over the things I can't control

What makes me so bold is when I pass on things I've been told, lo and behold

I find, sometimes, people just don't want to hear me speak

I guess without a license to teach, I lose my freedom of speech

But I would breach my contract with God if I didn't try to keep spirits flying

Even though many times I want to give up, if I said otherwise, I'd be lying

It's all about my heart, my passion, my start to my end

My soul won't rest until I have helped the world's transformation begin

I've Got a Weapon

I know some people may laugh
When they sarcastically ask if my weapon's on my hip or the dash
Because I don't seem like the one to carry a tech
But something is necessary for me to gain respect
Some try to warn me, "Don't use that in front of people."
I'm too smart to get caught, plus it's completely legal
And I'm not the only one to have one, I've even heard about a few at work
No wonder I'm always getting warned about someone else getting hurt
Even with that said, it still does not make me worry
Because as powerful as my weapon is, it hasn't caused anyone to get buried
But then again, maybe I'm wrong
Maybe the use of it will cause mankind not to last very long
Some might say it will help get rid of the weak
And everyday will be survival of the fittest on our neighborhood streets
And although my weapon always remains invisible
It does not mean its effectiveness is ever dismissible
And when I use it, best believe it's used intellectually
My weapon is my mind….and I promise, you do not want to mess with me

Love's Journey

As a man, we search for a woman who will somehow make us better
That will complete us
But that, @ times seems almost unrealistic because it seems women are all playing some sick and sadistic game
Trying to see how much we can take
How much we can deal with
And then, @ the end of it all, we are the losers
We have been taken farther away from our goals than we were when we initially started
With every ending relationship, we are robbed of @ least a little bit of who we were
Becoming a new person every single time
Sometimes we become better
Sometimes we become worse
But we're always different
@ times, it's almost as if during the relationship, we stand on the balcony of betrayal
Not knowing how we got there
Not knowing why we're there
Not ready to give up, but not necessarily knowing if we want to continue living through the struggle
And as we try to figure things out, women like to make the decision for us

They push us over the edge, hoping we won't survive the transition from the emotional high to the emotional lows

The crazy thing is, we always swear the "last one" has us more prepared for the "next one"

But it never seems to be the case

We are still almost always caught off guard

Well, I know I am

I never want to think the woman I'm with has the ability to hurt me

But she always does

More times than not, when a relationship has reached the end of its cycle, I find myself questioning who I am (again)

Questioning why I'm so blind that I can't see when I'm about to fall for the same things all over again

Questioning if I'm so dumb that maybe I just don't know any better

Perhaps I'm just so in love with the idea of being in love, I'm willing to look like a fool

And if such is the case, I guess I'm okay with that

See, nothing worth having should come easy to you

If it did, we may not see the actual value of it

So, I'll continue putting my heart out there until I find the woman who deserves it

The one who will keep it

Who will nourish and take care of it

And when that happens, I'll know the journey I took to make it to her…..

No matter how difficult

No matter how lengthy….

I'll know it was all worth it

Sure, I've been hurt more times than I would care to remember

We all have

But you know what?

I survived

I have been able to take what life has thrown at me and still pushed forward

We all know what doesn't kill us ultimately makes us stronger

So, when I finally reach my emotional destination, I'll know the journey would have me strong enough to actually be able to handle it

The Pressure

How would you feel if you didn't have a home?
No job, no money, and bill collectors won't leave you alone
The moans of your kids are all you hear
Permanent tears in your eyes, so you can't see clear
And your friends' lives, well they're basically the same
So there's nobody to help, nobody to blame
You pray everyday asking for nothing but a job
You get no reply, so you're losing faith in God
Every single day, you're feeling even more pressure
You wanna go to the store, but your wallet won't let ya
Everything says "stop," ain't no positive signs
Ain't no JJ Evans, so won't be no "Good Times"
And you're stuck with…the pressure

Hope in a Bottle

My friend told me he was addicted to cigarettes 'cause his life had already gone up in smoke
He said he had so many court orders that, in the sea of troubles, he couldn't stay afloat
He felt alone with hardly any friends and far too many foes
So it seems everyday he dies a little and he can't cope
Dreams, to him, are unrealistic, so he has no hope
And forget a paddle, he's up the creek without a boat
He was a writer, so he wrote the world a note
It said how he could no longer stomach his problems because he had already choked
And he could only breathe if everyone saw him go
So with a bottle full of pills and an empty house
He looked in his mirror as he poured the contents into his mouth
As he started to get drowsy, his mind took him back
To happier times before his vision faded to black
His legs became unstable before his body dropped to the floor
His spirit still partially wanted to live, but the physical being couldn't struggle through life anymore
He tried to live as God requested, but knew he was dying in sin
He hoped his death would make others happy, and in turn, put him in God's good graces again

But that was something he would never know

He just laid there as he died…really…slow

Alphabetic Perfection

Always on my case, not lettin' me rest
Because I wanna quit whenever I get too stressed
Cautious actions are thrown out of the door (and)
Denying responsibilities is something she won't stand for
Extracting the best out of whatever I do
Foolish behavior normally, but not around you
Greatness is the only thing that's expected (she)
Has my back constantly and for that she'll forever be respected
Ignorance is not bliss, not in my case
Jacob realizes that she could never be replaced
Killing me with kindness each and every day
Loving life, and I love the fact that she is that way
Mentally, she's on the same level as me
Never has any girl made me feel so free
Opposing forces don't want to see us together (a)
Persistent mind and you're like, "whatever"
Quietly, you make me better than I knew I could be (without)
Resistance I apply everything that you teach
Sustaining a level of perfection that's truly unmatched (constantly)
Testing me just to see how I react

Understands that I, by far, am not a perfect man
Venturing out of her way to lend a helping hand
Without giving it a second thought, she is by my side
(e)Xtraordinarily wonderful and truly one of a kind
Yielding to nothing that can stop her progress (and a)
Zealous attitude is the reason for her success

The Future

At times I sit back and think about a life I have yet to see
While trying to envision what will happen to the future version of me
I see how certain people will become top priority in my world
And how I would gladly give my life in exchange for my little girl's
I picture me watching the game on Sunday and turning around because, on my shoulder I felt a tap
It was my beautiful daughter asking if she can sit on my lap
I quickly turn down the volume of the game
So I could clearly hear her express the thoughts running through her inquisitive little brain
"Daddy, how did you and Mommy meet?"
Her mom poked her head in expecting to hear something sweet
"Ask me no questions, I'll tell you no lies,
I fell in love with your mother when I saw the view from behind."
Because I used those words, I knew more explaining would be needed
So as my daughter chuckled, with my words I proceeded
"It wasn't her butt, it was her strut. She walked with a level of confidence that was hard to achieve.
That's why my heart sank when I saw her starting to leave."
"So, what did you do, Dad?" She excitedly asked
"'At first I did nothing, I just let her walk past."
As we discussed the moment that changed my life

We were finally blessed with the presence of my wife

"But then your father approached me before I got into my car.

I saw him out of the corner of my eyes and hoped he wouldn't let me get too far."

"Did he ask you out, Mommy?" "Yes, he sure did."

"And a few years later, we were happily married and blessed with our own little kid."

I could tell by the look in my favorite ladies' eyes

Recalling that moment made them both want to cry

But alas, none of the happiness was for real

And being alone in reality brought back a pain I didn't want to feel

Although it saddens me when my visions start to fade

It keeps me inspired for when I am finally able to live through brighter days

The dreams and visions may not be real, but they still can be fun

They just make me run away from my past and towards the days to come

Mathematics

The sum of my actions shows I'm above average
I live with hopes and dreams of one day living a life that's lavish
If you multiply what I say, by those words that are unheard
You gain more than common knowledge, you get powerful words
When I subtract all negativity from my daily existence
I'm left with a man who is overcome with persistence
The root of being jovial comes from the spirit of God within
And using my tools: a notepad and a pen
I know a large percentage of my words won't equal to tons of extra cash
Because some will see positive words and they will skim right past
If you add up everything I said before
It will equal who I am; nothing less, nothing more

Road to Redemption

They say the H in Spanish is silent, but let me give you a case when it was not
I met a man on the bus named Hector, who not out of flyness, but out of anger said, "This is why I'm hot."
As an elder, he had my respect, so I paid attention even though I didn't know him
He told me the story of how he lost both arms
And had trouble holding his notebook of previously written poems
Actually, he didn't tell me, he had me go into his backpack, so I could grab the notebook and read his words aloud
And what started off as a conversation between two people ended up being me reciting his work for a crowd
And I was proud, even though I was also scared to death
But I knew his words were powerful, so I spoke them as if I was using my last breath
It started… "How does a man stay sane when he isn't allowed to see his daughter?
How can I keep vengeance off of my mind when I've seen both my mother and wife get slaughtered?"
I paused. "No need to stop, son, you're doing fine."
So I took a deep breath and continued to read his words as if they were actually mine

Ding! Ding!
Before I could get actual words out, the ringing let me know we had reached what was going to be my final destination
I took my eyes temporarily off the notebook, saw nobody moved, so I continued with only the slightest bit of hesitation
"When I was a little boy, I thought I could be famous,
but in the country of Cuba, I was a nobody, just one of the nameless.
I saw everyone in my country was being overrun with depression,
so at the age of 10, coming to the magical land known as the US became my obsession.
It became almost all I could think of, the only thing I could conceive,
and though I had never been to America, from my homeland I had to leave.
Me living my days out deprived was something I didn't want to believe.
I thought of many plans and moved towards them intensely, never casually.
I was disappointed to find imagination tends to move faster than reality.
I am 15 now, and still find myself stuck.
If it weren't for bad, I wouldn't have any luck,
but I am not giving up! That's what I kept telling myself.
As much as I wanted to reach out, there was nobody to help.
More time passed and now I'm 20.
My life's solutions are scarce, but my problems are plenty.
Darkness surrounds me, there seems to be no escape.

Every ounce of my existence has been overcome with hate.
I had thoughts of a greater destiny, but I was now thinking obscurity had to be my ultimate fate."
I looked up for a moment, giving myself a chance to clear my throat
I was getting very emotional and I could tell he was emotionally going for broke
"Please continue…..we want to hear where this goes…."
I wanted to stop, but I threw my desire to the side and continued the show.
"I was ready to give up on everything, ready to die,
but then an angel on earth passed right in front of my eyes.
I suppose she sensed I was feeling like less than a man,
so without even knowing me, she gently grabbed a hold of my hand.
Momentarily, I forgot where I was and how bad I wanted to leave.
All I could think about was convincing this woman she needed to be with me.
She said 'I know what you're thinking, so let me stop you before you start.
There's no need to say anything because I only walked over because you had already have stolen my heart.'
"Awwwww!" was all I heard from those in the crowd
It was the same thing I was thinking, they just happen to have said it aloud
Pride was beaming from the man like sun rays to the earth
It seemed this was one of the few times he felt good about his worth
But then he put his head down because he knew what was next
"Before he continues reading, I have something I must confess…"

He hadn't said much to this point, so I was a bit surprised
And became even more so when I saw the tears in his eyes
"Now we get back to a part of my life I tried to block out of my mind.
This is the part when I was lost, and happiness, I could no longer find."
Now I was nervous, I didn't know if I wanted to read
I had to put my feelings to the side as I was once again told to proceed
"I don't know how, but word got around that I was trying to leave,
so I was viewed as a problem by those who were far more important than me.
See, in America, you have many freedoms, such as freedom of speech.
At home, it didn't even seem like we had freedom to breathe.
I knew the danger, so I denied what they said.
For if I spoke the truth, I knew I'd be dead.
My parents always told me if something was worth having, it was worth fighting.
And to keep control of my emotions, they recommended I started writing.
It helped from the time I was a kid, to the time I had a wife.
Whenever I was emotionally blind, it somehow helped me gain sight.
However, I stopped for a while, after my daughter was born.
When the doctor delivered bad news and our hearts felt like they had literally been torn.
I tried to hold my tears inside, but my wife couldn't do the same.
They said she had some kind of tumor growing on her brain.
We couldn't afford any kind of surgery, we were far too poor.

The doctor didn't care, so he basically pointed us to the door.
Now we had to take care of a child who would have very special needs.
I prayed daily for the Lord to help us find a way to pay for our hospital fees.
Soon, I had to have a conversation with my wife.
It had to be one of the most difficult ones I ever had in my life.
We decided it would be best for our child's life if we gave her up for adoption.
Before that, we tried many ideas, many mental concoctions …"
The people on the bus were still attentive, but Hector knew they had to go
So he advised me to skip forward a bit in his 'reality show'
He said I should move about three pages towards the end of his book
I did as requested as the travelers continued to look
"I don't know where you want me to start."
Hector looked before he said, "Just follow your heart."
I did just that as I turned one more page
Hoping my actions wouldn't fill him with rage
He smiled as I looked around our 'mobile venue'
He nodded his head, letting me know it was okay to continue
"…So there we were; me, my wife, and mom.
I was told somebody was going to die, but I tried to remain calm.
So, you want to leave your home, you want to only think about self?
Now, at least one of you is not going to live, so when is your precious America going to help?

The time moved in slow motion, my whole life flashed.

I had to relive my decisions while facing my past.

I went from my childhood to when I had a child of my own.

Thought about how the place where my wife and I lived could never be my daughter's home.

I pictured notepads, scrap paper, and everywhere else I used to write.

I thought about my mother and when my dad lost his life.

My thoughts were interrupted when the man, once again, began to speak.

He saw my backpack and asked if I was one to teach.

'I am no professor, I just scribbled down some words.'

Then his face frowned as if he thought that was absurd.

So, you must really like to write?

But would you choose words over your wife or the woman who gave you life?

As much as I loved to express how I felt emotionally,

there was no way I would sacrifice their lives so I could continue writing poetry.

He asked again while looking me in my face.

Without saying anything, he could tell I would go through great lengths to keep them both safe.

Are you willing to give up anything to show your strength as a man?

I nodded as he asked me how good of a writer could I be if I had no arms or hands.

With my arms and hands tied, I knew what he was about to do, and the screams coming from my mother and wife let me know they did too.

Yes, I lived my life trying to help others, so this was unfair,

but I loved those women more than life itself, so honestly, I didn't care.

So, using an old, rusty saw, the stranger became a man of his word.

The ladies couldn't watch, but I'm sure they heard.

I tried not to yell as my hands and arms became separated from my body.

Although I was in pain, it was the pain of those women I was more concerned with stopping."

Hector cleared his throat, making me stop reading what was written.

"I know you want to know how the rest was written with no arms, you think my story is conflicting."

I hadn't thought about it, but he started to explain.

"What I used to do with my hands, I started doing with my feet, that's why the rest of the writing will change."

I was already amazed, but now my admiration was raised.

He had a slight hint of a smile as he told me to continue on the page.

I wanted Hector to receive all of his glory

So I did what I was told and jumped right back into the story.

"Do you see what happens when you want to leave?

That was the question he asked as he looked directly at me.

I thought that's where my pain would stop,

until I heard the sound of a gun being cocked.

I was ready to go, so I took a deep breath,

but he chose to use the bullets to bring my loved ones to their death.

He figured it would be more fun to torture me, so he wanted me to watch them die.

I was upset, angry, sad and confused…. I couldn't even cry.

I no longer knew the concept of life; I started pounding my head on the concrete floor.

Whatever I thought the meaning of life was previously, I no longer knew anymore.

He looked at me and asked, 'Do you think you can die that easy?'

He picked my body up and said, 'Now we must stop the bleeding.'

He pulled my limp body away and at my family I had to look back.

I wished I could have killed myself, then my vision faded to black.

'We no longer want you here, so off to America you go.

If you ever try to come back, we'll make sure your daughter won't get to grow.'

I was forced to do what I thought was my dream for so long.

Even though I soon found myself floating in a raft with five others, I felt incredibly alone.

My mind made me think of ways to change the past,

but reality kept setting in, so what I imagined could never last.

Finally, I made it to the country that I now called my home.

Constantly dreaming about a daughter that I would never know.

There was nothing else written, no other text

So like an inquisitive child, I asked, "What happened next?"

"In my mind, I pictured my child growing. I pictured her independent style.

I imagined the kids she may have, I pictured their smiles.

I don't know her exact age, but she would be around thirty.

So I pray she is happy, removed the surgery, and there is no more hurting."

Right then the bus paused, I guess we were making another stop

"Recently I heard she moved to America, working in that building, right near the top.

So everyday I ride this bus, hoping to confirm the rumor.

Really hoping to see her once more before I die because my heart and head hurts like I am carrying her tumor."

Then he cried as he moved the remaining part of his arms towards his head

"In a matter of months, I'll probably be dead.

So, I'll live out my days on this land."

And right then, most of the people started to stand

I guess they had finally reached their end of the line

Most of them thanked Hector for sharing his time

But one lady just stood still, with tears streaming down her face and falling off of her chin

The bus was about to start moving, but then she started moving again

She said nothing, she just moved closer

The tears were still flowing as she put her hand on his shoulder

She said some Spanish words that I didn't understand

Right before she showed Hector her hand.

She pointed out a ring, and yes, it was very nice

But then Hector yelled, "That's the ring that belonged to my wife!"

"Yes. It appeared in a box that was sitting in front of my door.

It had a note inside that started off by saying, 'I can't carry the guilt anymore.'

Then, the note said my mom was wearing the ring the day she died.

The person who wrote the note said he was partially responsible, and it was killing him inside.

He said he didn't pull the trigger, but he was there to watch.

He let it continue, when he could have had it stopped.

When her body hit the ground and my father was being taken out of the room,

the joy he used to feel from the tragedy of others was quickly turning into gloom.

He said without giving more details and forcing my mind to visualize things I shouldn't see,

he apologized again and said the ring should be with me."

When she stopped talking, Hector put his head down as an epiphany occurred

He didn't have to say anything more because we all knew it was her

It was his daughter, the only family he still had

And after so many years of not hearing it, she simply called him "Dad"

I, unlike them, found myself dumbfounded and baffled

I finally exited the bus smiling; knowing Hector's road to redemption had finally been traveled

Remember

I remember when there once was a time I used to dream at night
I imagined being successful, choosing to live life right
But then came the time when good left my mind
The day I met drugs and our lives became intertwined
She was like nirvana tucked neatly in a bad
Presenting me with happiness that I thought I could never have
At least I thought I had found a brand new friend
But the beginning of our relationship was the start of my end
Every time we met up, we skipped the foreplay
Got right into the action; we both liked it better that way
She didn't ever speak, so I never complained
And I swore to myself she wouldn't cause me to change
The day I entered her life, was the day I became unprotected
That was why the rest of my life would soon become neglected
She soon became dangerous, filling me with sorrow
And I didn't know if I wanted to live if I couldn't see her on tomorrow
She could spring new life into me or cause me to fall into my life's winter
But she never did me wrong…
… at least that's how I remember

Be

I could be something good or be something bad

I could be the reason for happiness or the reason you're mad

I can be a lover or be your friend

I can be your beginning until we both reach our end

I can be a shoulder to cry on when you need it

I can be your one true friend once you've succeeded

I can be the one to buy you things like diamond rings

Or simply be your inspiration, the reason you sing

I can be a student, always eager to learn

I can patiently wait until it's finally my turn

I can be one to go fast or one to go slow

I can be the reason you want to leave, but the reason you can't go

I can be the one who walks you down the aisle

But first I want to be the one that makes you smile

I can be the one with whom you want to dance

Be the one captivated by your beauty, totally caught in your trance

I can be the one with whom you build your life

And in turn, you can be my wife

I can be 'near-perfect' but still make mistakes

Go from the bottom to the top, that's why life is great

Out of all the things I can try to be

The most difficult of all is to just...be...me

Only in America

We don't have the money for the poor to be fed
But we always find it easy to pay for bloodshed
Our former presidents loved sending us to war
But they never really explained what we were going for
They talked about operations of liberation
But there actions were causing the loss of the lives of several generations
But I can't say anything bad because they were our presidents
The American leader doesn't have to be smart, that certainly was evident
It seems they just have to be an American resident
Who's able to elect themselves from lies and negligence
The thoughts going through my brain
Constantly drive me insane
But I'll try not to complain
About the biggest hustlers to ever get into the game
Who gained fame mainly because of their names
Dang! Are we so blind we can't see the bigger picture
In many ways their ideology was similar to Hitler's
Willing to kill so they can make a profit
Knowing nobody was powerful enough to try to stop it
But America can still be great: not because of our leadership, but in spite of it

I'm More Interested..

Of course I want to know what you have to say

But I'm more interested in how you got that way

The words that leave your lips are one thing, but I want to know why the others were stopped

There had to be some importance in your thoughts, so why were they blocked?

And I love the way you look because you can tell you spent time applying your makeup

But I'm more interested in seeing how you look when you wake up after a night spent with Jacob

And a dude would be a fool to not enjoy seeing you in that dress that stops about 4 inches above the knee

But I'm more interested in the mystery of what I can't see

You're successful and independent, but you only allow most to know part of your story

I'm interested in becoming the man to whom you expressed what others end up ignoring

Eve was made for Adam, now I understand

Clearly I'm more interested in how I can be your man

My intuition says my disposition in life is solely because you're missin'

So I'm curious to see if you've even listened

The past is just that, and was was wrong then won't all of a sudden get

right

But I'm more interested in the future and how we'll spend the rest of our

lives

Job Description

Somebody once asked me "What do you do?"

I wanted to tell him that I do things on a daily basis that would one day change a nation

But instead, I replied, " I take notations."

"So, you're a secretary?"

He laughed

I guess he did so 'cause my job didn't fit his plan

Either that or he thought it wasn't the type of job that should be held by a man

"You must not have been able to find anything else to do."

I shook my head while saying, "Let me explain something to you.

As long as it's an honest living, you have no right to look down on my job."

"But all you do is take messages."

"Yeah, but I take them for God."

Immediately his face changed shape, he was no longer happy

He no longer felt he was in the position to laugh at me

But there were no apologies, at least not yet

He just seemed a little uneasy, a tad bit upset

"So I take it that was not something you expected."

"No, and I'm sorry if you feel disrespected."

I would have been much worse than he

If I didn't accept his apology

But I had to dig deep within me

To clear the cataracts of my emotional vision to see

If I want to be respected, I have to respect others equally

If I didn't, I would be living hypocritically

"When you said you take messages for God, what did you mean?"

"I meant, I'm a writer and for these words, I'm a fiend.

But the things I write, they can't came from man.

I feel my words are being written by God's hand."

Now he smiled, vocally at a momentary loss

"I bet not too many people would think of disrespecting your boss."

"No, not normally, but sometimes I meet people like you.

Those who disrespect at first, but then change their tune."

He was humbled to the point of silence, so he decided it was time for him

to leave

I guess God used our conversation to send a message that was obviously

received

See, no job of honor should be ridiculed

For no person is better than the next

The Lord will all make play the part of fools

To show we need to keep our egos in check

Your paycheck can be in the millions, but how much love are you giving

When God looks at your life's resume, will He say you match what's on

the job description?

Easily Ignored

As a child, whenever you ask a certain type of question, you're told to stay in your place

So you stay quiet

But how do you really know where your place is if you never question anything?

Again, you only do what you're told….@ least for the time being

But at some point, someone needs your help

They need your input

They need your opinion

But because of years of being told to be quiet and to not ask anything, you choose to remain silent

You would rather be quiet than continue to be ignored

You now feel your silence is just a chance for everybody else to get it together

Or maybe that's just me

Too many times people have said I'm too quiet

I have been told that many people think I'm arrogant when they first meet me

They believe I'm stuck up

But like many people do with my verbal and nonverbal words, I ignore them

As far as being quiet goes, maybe I no longer want to share all of my thoughts with everyone

The crazy thing is, once I start talking, I'm told I talk too much

When such is the case, what am I to do?

Should I ignore ignorance, or argue with fools?

Either way, it will eventually come back to haunt me

So, I revert back to what I was told as a child

I stay quiet and I stay in my place

Just for everyone else's happiness and amusement

You want someone to blame?

I'll be that person

You need a person to point the finger at?

Well, here I am

When it's all said and done, I'll take your negativity

In fact, I'll probably smile as it forces me to move forward

As it helps me to progress

And I'll be a lot of things

But no longer will I be easily ignored

Acting In Confidence

Contusions from illusions seem to wreck my brain
Crashing into a wall of confusion, it's all driving me insane
The same things I try to maintain are the ones that got me here
But yet I continue to battle because the unknown causes fear
Here is the place and I guess the time is now
We all want to do better, but very few know how
Every day is a war, every second is a struggle
I don't normally question my strength, but I may lack the muscle
Not physically, but mentally and it gets harder when people won't let me be
I'm surrounded by clouds of negativity and a lack of clarity makes the solution hard to see
Spiritually, I don't know how much longer any of us can take it
We should be receiving lifetime achievement Academy Awards the way we all continue faking it
Acting as if we're getting 20 million a check
When all the while we're lying just to gain respect
And if we lie to get something, is it even something we truly deserve
If we try to speak the truth, will we even get heard

My Block

On my block, there's only love for the streets
And life, well, it's very hard to keep
On my block, waking can be a chore
Everyday is a gift, but sometimes you just don't want it anymore
On my block, guns are used to rob people of their cars
And nobody cares who you say you are
Oh, you say you're a cop, then they just may stop
Only temporarily, until the guns start to pop
On my block, folks go to jail often
Either that, or they get free rides to cemeteries in their coffins
On my block, folks ain't got no friends
And the only thing they care about is stacking their ends
On my block, things are far from great
But unlike some others, (my life), I appreciate
On my block, the outlook for the future doesn't look good
But I love everything about it, 'cause that's my hood
And my block may not be the best place to live
But I'm gonna make it out, 'cause I (try to) remain positive

Weary

Folks are getting tired of me, I can feel their spite

I sometimes feel love in the day, but at night I must fight

To go through the darkness and find the light

(Within) I feel my pen sometimes is the only friend I have

And my emotions will become clearer once I perfect my craft

The last thing I hope to accomplish before I leave this place

Is leaving my family physically, financially, and emotionally safe

I want to have kids who will carry on my name

Children who will learn from my mistakes and not do the same

Because change is not always bad

Especially if others benefit and get things I never had

And my wife, she'll be down for whatever

Stunningly beautiful and extremely clever

But for now, those are only dreams

Of a far off place that I can't see

On a road that I am currently unable to reach

Desiring to pass on lessons I can't yet teach

But's that's life.

And in spite of my downfalls, I will reach glory

And leave a trail of written emotions that will ultimately tell my story

Even when I reach the day of my demise

I'll always expect greatness, so when it's achieved, I won't be surprised

In the end, I know I'll be filled with my emotional scars

But at some point I hope to realize life truly wasn't hard

Since I lived a difficult life, I'll be able to die with ease

And only if God's will is done will I truly be able to rest in peace

Misconceptions

One of the misconceptions of pain
Is that the gloominess of rain will overshadow better days
But hey, the rainbow that comes behind the clouds is what we forget
It's because of that, our optimistic views normally give way to those that are the opposite
God does things that show no matter the darkness, there will always be light
No matter how far left you've strayed, you can always get right
As I've gotten older & my lifetime's forecast has seemingly grown colder
My ability to inspire through words has somehow grown bolder
I confess at times I fall into a state of unrest
But I don't give up because I know God is providing a test
One that, no matter how difficult, *if* we follow Him, we won't have the ability to fail
He shows us if we never struggle, we can't truly enjoy when things go well
For me, the rain from the clouds is now like soaking in God's reign
We can't expect to grow if we don't endure some pain

After Elza

No more life, no more joy, and no more laughter
All that was before, this is the after
They always say you don't know what you've got until it's gone
You don't feel by yourself until someone leaves you alone
Such is what I'm going through today
A few years after I found my great uncle passed away
See, being away from family can truly hurt
Especially when you find one has left the earth
Is it fair? I guess it is because it's God's plan
Now my uncle is going into the light while holding the Lord's hand
Sure, physically he's now out of our sight
But still, we have to thank God for his life
So, the next time I play dominoes, I may look towards the clouds
And start smiling suddenly, but he'll know what it's about
But then he may actually help me win
At least until we're able to play against each other again
I love you Uncle E, I'm going to try and keep a smile on my face
If for no other reason, just for knowing you're in a better place

(Untitled)

May the hand of God continue to bless

When the ways of the world continue to stress

People will always try, but we need to make sure they always fail

In trying to make you lose happiness whenever things are going well

The world is not always filled with a group of beloved friends

Many people like to see the joy of others come to an end

Release your feelings and try to never hold a grudge

Anger is a cataract of deception making us lose sight of what we're dreaming of

We all fall down because nobody has perfect luck

But it is never failure if you continue getting up

Only you know what you're truly capable of

And when you want to give up, remember God is love

He is everything we aspire to be

And when we learn that, we will remain happy

Life's Tribulations

The trials and tribulations of my so-called life
Have me questioning my morals and if I'm living right
Does my life have a purpose? Right now, I don't even know
How can I hold my head up if I feel so low?
Conflicts and complications have me battling myself
And my foolish pride hardly ever allows me to ask for help
My inside, well, it's also filled with scars
And I never would have thought living would be this hard
It seems like everyday I lose sight of another one of my dreams
I question if anything positive will ever be meant for me
I smile sometimes, just to keep from crying
I sometimes say I'm happy when I know I'm lying
My sanity, well, that soon may be lost
Because happiness is expensive and I can never seem to pay the cost
At times, I want to throw in the towel and end my fight
But I can't experience joy if I don't live life

To Dad

Growing up, my dad wasn't the type of man to hold my hand
And it was one of the things I couldn't understand
But looking back, I see it was a form of tough love
And when it comes to life's stumbling blocks, I can now rise above
Some of the same things that cause other people to trip and fall
And with my short stature, I can still stand tall
Back then, it seemed like he was being mean
When he simply was preparing me for a view of life that had yet to be seen
On Saturdays, it used to hurt when he was at work and couldn't play
He would tell me bills couldn't wait and I would see one day
I see now, and I'm glad I wasn't given anything for free
'Cause the struggles and hard times are what help made me
Now I'm at a point where I want to help
By passing on lessons to my brother that I couldn't learn myself
Although he's young, he's not a kid
We just have to pray he's okay with the man he is
Whatever he thinks, one thing is clear
The lessons of Greg Grovey, Sr. helped us get here
Dad, you have my love, respect, and I appreciate your guidance
And through my life, the man you helped raise is what I hope you take the most pride in

Black

One of the definitions of black is the absence of light
And in the game of life, some would say being born Black was my first strike
That ain't right, but they say it's true
'Cause we're "wicked and gloomy," at least…that's definition number two
It's one thing to be Black, but I'm also a Black male
Which means at birth, I fit the description of most of the people in jail
If I ever decided I needed a permanent place to roam, the government is set up to help make prison my home
With thousands of roommates and correctional officers that won't leave me alone
And speaking of officers, it's if the roles have been switched
Now some of the most politically correct are those outside of politics
Yes, it's true that some people in the hood do lie, cheat, and steal
But they seem more conscious of consequences because they *don't* have a proverbial license to kill
No, that only comes when you have white skin and a badge
When you can put fifty bullets in a person, then complain about the bullets you thought they might have had
I guess the boys in blue don't want their career to flop
So they beat and kill people so they can reach the top
Sometimes I wonder how they can sleep at night

Nowadays it seems like they get promoted when they can end a life
Don't get me wrong; I'm not advocating any violence towards them
Because regardless of the motives, a sin is a sin
Although they judge my worth while on earth, they all will eventually answer to someone higher
They may be a master of deceit while living, but after life they'll just be viewed as a liar
Then at the pearly gate, they will be asked about their mind state
And asked if they were the type to hate someone simply because of their race
They say no, knowing they are a fraud
Hoping their lies will be believable enough to fool God
Since they're not, in so many words, their life is a wrap
And vengeance will be served when they're reincarnated as someone Black

My Perspective

"They" say ignorance is bliss

It was said one of early definitions of a n****r is an ignorant person

Is that why us Black folks seem so happy to call each other that word

Either that, or we just don't know any better

We get mad when judgmental America creates stereotypes

But we fuel what they say by wearing gold chains that go from our necks to the pants that are hanging so far below our waist, we might as well not be wearing any

We disrespect each other with our 'terms of endearment' almost every time we converse with one another

But then, we get mad when someone outside of our circle says the same thing our *friend* did

I know it's somehow acceptable for Black people to ask, "What's up my n****r?" but it's wrong for whites

Why? Maybe it's acceptable to say your Black friend is ignorant as long as you are Black, too

In that case, I'm ignorant to how that makes any kind of sense

Don't get me wrong, I completely understand about the historical content of the word and the pain associated with it

With the things our ancestors had to endure, it's no wonder we get so upset we're ready to fight when white people let the word leave their mouths

But how do we think our ancestors would feel if they heard us call each other the same word that served as the last thing they heard before they were unjustly killed because of racism?

Just something to ponder

And it goes beyond blacks; males and females do the same thing with each other

Men call their friends dogs, women calls theirs a b***h

But each gender gets mad when the other says the same thing

I be dog gone, this mess doesn't make any sense

Now, I've heard the argument, "Well, we didn't create the negative word, we just took it and turned it into something good."

None of us created stupidity either, so how do we plan on changing that into something good?

Again, just something to think about

When you think about it, "life" is just a four-letter word

It can sometimes feel good to just say, when other times, saying it can bring a sense of depression

I guess the positivity of the word, like all the others, just depend on how you look at it

As least, that's my perspective

The Story of Beauty

Her head was covered as if she was shielding her thoughts from the undeserving world

I was intrigued

Her eyes… they showed me the goodness of her soul

She smiled with a smile that was bright enough to put the sun to shame

Her body was the masterpiece every artist wished they could create

If perfection could be personified it would be her

Her voice….was that of an angel

Her personality was like puzzle pieces, fitting perfectly with mine

I hoped she was a dream because in reality, she was beyond me

I was undeserving and I knew she was aware of it

She glanced at me as if in slow motion

My heart skipped a beat as we moved closer to each other

"Hi, my name is…."

She stopped me

"I already know who you are. You are the one I prayed for."

I looked around because I knew she couldn't have been talking to me

She smiled again

"Do you believe in love @ 1st sight?" She asked.

"I don't know. Does it count if this is the first time I've actually seen love?"

She didn't move

For a moment, it was as if I was holding her heart hostage

I didn't want to let it go, but it wasn't mine

At least, not yet

She put her hand on my heart

It was like she instantly knew my past

Like she could feel that my heart had been broken into a million pieces;

only to be stitched up and broken all over again

"You don't have to worry about that anymore."

I don't know why, but I trusted her

I trusted her like I had known her all of my life, when in reality, I still

didn't even know her name

My phone rang

It was terrible timing, but I felt I needed to answer it

She removed her hand as I removed the phone from my pocket

I recognized the number, but I couldn't yet remember from where

I pondered as the call reached its 3rd ring

"Hello."

I finally answered, but it was like the person on the other end wanted me

to see what it was like to wait

It was no problem for me to repeat myself

"Hello."

My ears heard nothing, but my mind acted as if I had been told life-

altering news

Now, there was a dial tone on the other end

I checked my call log so I could see the number and possibly call the person back

I was left speechless when I remembered the number was that of my grandmother

See, my "Big Mama's " sun had set a while ago

Sure, the call could have been just a coincidence, but what where the odds of that?

"That was…….my grandmother," I said.

"That's nice. Has it been a while since you all have spoken?"

"…..Yeah."

"Well, you shouldn't be talking to me, you should call her back."

That's when I lost control of my emotions

Tears were pouring out of my eyes as if I had to personally refill the world's oceans

"What's wrong?"

Her concern was genuine, but I didn't know if I should tell her

Maybe the silly idea I had running around in my head would scare her away

Then again, maybe it wouldn't

Now, I had to find out

"My grandmother has been gone for a while, but this was her number."

I pointed @ the most recent call

I actually thought she would leave, but she didn't

"So, what do you think that means?" She asked.

"I think Big Mama is letting me know I should give you a chance."

I smiled as she wiped the tears away from my face and gave me a hug

"Oh, I would have loved her!"

She was right and didn't even know it

She would have loved her, just like everyone else did

I stepped back and just looked @ her

…..Amazed

…….Astonished

…….Still not believing she was real, still not believing the situation was real

We didn't say anything else about the phone call

There was no need to

"I'm Jacob, by the way."

I felt it was way past time she knew who I was

She responded by telling me her name

She held my hand as we both walked towards the exit

We caught the eyes of several people as we moved

I'm sure they looked @ us & saw a couple that had been together for years

And that's how I felt

Our connection was surreal

"It figures," she said.

I let go of her hand without even realizing what I was doing

"What figures?"

I admit I was a bit upset when I asked, and I'm sure that came across in my tone

"I know what you're thinking, but it's nothing bad, I promise," she said.

I heard those words before

They normally preceded the beginning of my relationship's end

"Okay, please explain."

She inhaled and exhaled slowly before speaking again

"I just meant….well, it figured your name would be a biblical one. I prayed that God would allow me to see who I have been looking for…. And honestly, I believe that's you."

I was left speechless

I'm sure a statement like that would have made many guys run away

Scared

Lost

Not me, though

I had actually been looking forward to the day when a woman told me I was what she was looking for

I honestly thought it would never happen, though

But I had heard, on more than one occasion, I was a bit abnormal

Having the ability to be me has always been one of the few things I have always liked about myself

I digress, though

"That has to be one of the nicest things anyone has ever said to me."

As those words left my lips, I was thinking about things past girlfriends told me

How, at the time, they made me feel like we would be together forever

But this didn't feel the same

I didn't know why

I couldn't tell if it was skepticism

Or overly ambitious expectations

Or perhaps it was both

Maybe it was part of me not actually allowing me to be happy while battling the other half of me for emotional supremacy

Who knew?

I certainly didn't

I felt myself doing something I had a habit of doing....

Over thinking

I was playing a good versus evil game of chess by myself and it seemed I wouldn't allow the good side to get anywhere near a checkmate

Why was that?

Maybe because 'good' had won several of my love battles in the past only to allow the evil to win the war

I guess my battered, bruised and scared heart didn't want to fight only to have the same outcome

But they say anything worth having is worth fighting for

Who are they, anyway?

And how do they seem to know everything about everybody else's life?

Wait!

What was I doing?

How long had I let my mind wonder?

Had my lack of focus on reality ruin a future I now may never reach?

Internally, I slapped myself

Bringing me back to the world I had to face

I had to take a moment to look @ her again

My lips quivered

"I just n-never would have thought……"

"Thought what?" She asked.

"I-I-I don't know, I just….."

Yeah, my words were so brilliant

So eloquent

So profound

It was no wonder I was alone

It wasn't because of my few moments of greatness

But because of my many moment of stupidity

"I know exactly what you mean, Jacob."

Wow!

I had heard my name said thousands, if not millions of times, but never had it sounded that good

Her few worlds lifted my self-esteem higher than the heavens she seemed to have descended from

"I have a question for you," she said.

"Ok. What's up?"

"Well, I know we just met, and I love your name, but can I call you 'Baby'?"

I smiled yet again

Life's crazy

You go your entire childhood wanting the people around to refer to and look @ you as an adult

But then you live your adult life searching for someone who will call you their baby

Another smile crept across my face before answering

"Of course! Why would that be an issue?"

"Well, sometimes… let's just say I wouldn't be surprised @ anything a guy would tell me," she said.

"Women have gotten me to that point, too," I replied.

"I guess we have to take it upon ourselves to mend the paths of each other's emotional pasts."

Her words were like those from the world's most brilliant poetic minds

I was inspired

Not inspired to be able to speak as she did

But inspired to be the one who continued to inspire her to speak

That was now one of my goals

"Where do we go from here?" She asked.

"There are no limitations when you and I are our only obligations."

I guess I could be a bit poetic

Or perhaps they were words I heard before in one of the songs I enjoyed listening to

Whatever the case, I didn't know how my words were received, though

So, I waited

Then, I received another hug and a kiss on the cheek

I felt like a six year old who had just received a personalized Valentine's Day card from the prettiest girl in class

Her actions were innocent

But I liked them

She gave me a sample of what heaven felt like

And it made me, eventually know I would want more

"So, do you think I can have your number?" I asked very nervously

I could only partially look her in her enchanting eyes as I asked

I still was unable to totally conquer my life-long fear of rejection

"That's so cute," she said.

"What?"

"The fact you're scared to ask me for my number as if I'm actually going to turn you down."

Yeah, it sounded a bit silly when she said it

It didn't take away from the fact I was actually still scared

Time passed and I not only had her number, but I also had her heart

It wasn't being held hostage this time, though

She handed it to me on a silver platter

She told me to be careful with it because it was fragile

She gave me happiness

And said we should both be thankful

For the happiness that was provided to me was simply the reciprocation of

what was being provided by her

Again, my heart skipped

Why?

Well, I guess I was always used to looking for love and I didn't really

know how to act now that I found it

Or maybe it found me

Yeah, that had to be it

I couldn't @ all be responsible for the dream that had become my reality

I wasn't really concerned with the technicalities of it all

In fact, there wasn't much I was concerned with

@ least not to the point of being stressed

Which is….well……let's just say it's different for me

Reliving everything makes me understand, once again, how fortunate I am

And just think……this is just the story of how everything started

Want to know how it all ends?

Well, I'll let you know if it actually does…..

Get By

The world is a minefield; you have to watch where you step
My mind's filled with potential that I haven't reached yet
I try to move in love, but I'm surrounded by hate
I try to live spiritually, but people keep testin' my faith
I'm trying to get by with my words and a backpack
It's 2009 and I get judged 'cause my skin's black
Blast back to a bleak section in our country's time
When my folks couldn't dream of getting' paid to rhyme
Most of my people struggle just to survive
And that was just 2005
(Look) I scream like that painting or song by Mike Jackson
We can talk a good game, but very few are about action
The lacerations from the whip are embedded from the time when we were slaves
But back then we seemed a lot more brave
If we had something to say, we take beatings and start riots
Now with free speech and lack of knowledge, we choose to remain silent
I get by with my words of optimism
If I no longer believe in the government, some say I lack patriotism
On the contrary, I still believe in the potential of the U-S of A
But it's because of its actions I choose to act this way
Some say I'm still young enough to have no reasons to complain

It's because of that same reason I have everything to gain

I have the blood of kings and queens running deep in my veins

So of course I want greatness, mediocrity drives me insane

The fast lane to richness is never legally open

That's the main reason why most of my people's spirits are broken

I'm chokin' on my own insecurities and obsessions

But at the same time I'm trying to learn, I'm also trying to teach the youth a few lessons

Like; happiness can't be paid for, it can only be earned

We all are destined for greatness, we just are waiting our turn

It's hard getting to the top, but very easy to get down

And if you do fall, will your friends still be around

Or will you find out they were only there for the paper

And when you become broke, will they find reasons to hate ya?

Sometimes, every day you wake up is the start of new tragedies

And because I speak the truth, some folks will stay mad at me

It's sad to see if you make comments without using your brain

You may be rich, but do the opposite and your career won't sustain

I hope and pray for the day when it won't be a lie

To say everything's okay and I know we'll get by

Letter to the Lord

My God:

I come to you a battered man

Bruised ego

Feeling crushed to my soul

Not knowing why, I find myself question my motives

Probably because I don't know what else to do

I cried, trying to get well

But the well has gone dry

No amount of water seems to be able to wash the pain away

So I swim

Struggling to swim upstream

Struggling to keep my head above water

Struggling in a battle with myself…..

Should I…..just give up?

I withdraw my question because I know giving up isn't something I can actually do

I don't have that option

I can't afford to let go of hope

My acceptance of failure may lead to more of the same

Not just from me, but from those around

Those future personalities that I will one day be responsible for

Those who look up to me, and in turn, those who inspire me to keep trying to do better

I know God won't close a door without also opening a window

So I search

Search through the seemingly infinite chaos known as my life

I know somehow the pain is just hiding the escape window I'm seeking

The ability to make it sometimes seems nonexistent, but I continue…..

I continue until I finally see the light bursting through the opportunistic window

Some actually fear the light

They don't want to be able to truly see everything around them

They would rather be left in the darkness

Some even say the light at the end of the tunnel means death

So they stray away from it

But not me

I'm different

To me the light equals life

And you know what?

I think I'm finally ready to live

(Untitled)

So, I guess you want me to recycle love like an older sibling's clothes
What will I decide? I guess only heaven knows
You say you are showing your love by the things you say
Then, your actions show you're actually thinking a completely different way
But hey, I guess it's human nature for you to change your mind
And it's not daylight savings, so I don't want to mess with time
@ least that's what my mind says, but then my heart…
Well, it doesn't want me to stop love before it even starts
Our love was a chess game, you were my queen
I was almost the pawn of your existence; willing to do anything
Now you've ended the game with a checkmate
And the consequence of your actions is me moving on to the next date
Life's great, at least, it is when you're free to do what you want to
I guess that is the rainbow after the rain of all the things I've gone through
I loved you, so don't ever get that twisted
But I didn't experience true happiness until our relationship no longer existed

I Am

I am the darkness

I am what you see when the disparities of the world seem to have you trapped in those negative situations

I am most happy when you are not

I love watching people struggle

And when you give up….well, I'll take credit for that

Your struggles make it feel as if you are in a cycle of pain that you will never escape from

Well, mission accomplished

All of the bad feelings you have ever had,

I bet you can find me somewhere near by

See, it's obvious you don't think very much about who you are

I think how you feel is justified

What do you have to offer the world? Nothing

Name one thing you're good for….you can't do it!

You are a wasted egg and the sperm it was fertilized by

The world would have been better off if you were never allowed to live in the first place

You are a pointless mass of nothingness

Your blood, flesh, and bones are pointless

But I love you, for your misery brings me joy

I am your self-doubt

And I dare you to kill me

Open Letter to Ms. Lady

I had to put down on paper some things I can't understand
Like how you can take all of this foolishness from boys, while claiming to be looking for a man
If you don't stand for something, you'll fall for anything
Which is why these dudes waste money on ice, but won't buy you a wedding ring
I can see it because I'm on the outside looking in
And as much as I try to move past it, I end up in the zone that's destined for friends
That's messed up! That's how I honestly feel
Pardon my lack of tact, but I'm just keeping it real
Maybe my honesty is what's holding me back
'Cause most dudes who are habitual liars get what they want and I find it hard to come to terms with that
Perhaps if I lied, then I'd be able to keep a chick
I'll tell her one thing and then do the opposite
Let me ask you something Ms. Lady, are you looking for a man with intellect
Or for the thug-type that likes treating you with disrespect
Judging by your actions, I think you like choice number two
So, it's kind of your fault negativity seems to follow you
I'm calling you Ms. Lady when I should refer to you as a little girl

When you grow up emotionally, maybe then you'll allow me to be a part of your world

Thinking outside of your norm may work because the concept alone can be viewed as crazy

But these are just my thoughts in an open letter to you, Ms. Lady

Tetris

I constantly find myself trying to fit together the pieces of my life

As hard as I try, sometimes they don't line up right

When I think I'm doing well, I find I'm actually doing bad

I try to clear things up, but some squares like to block my path

Even when that's taken care of, I'm still dealt an 'L'

I guess I have that to blame when things don't go well

Now my life is getting filled with pieces that won't fit

And I've already pushed the start button, so I guess I can't quit

They say life is a game, so I can't progress if I don't play

I just wish when I did, it didn't turn out this way

The game gets rough, and @ times I feel pathetic

But there is no way I'm gonna give up because unlike a game, life only

gives you one credit

'09 Revolution

We were brought to this country tied up in chains
Now in 2009, we're enslaved by the same 'thangs'
Only thing is, the chains don't belong to 'masa' no more
They belong to all of the owners of the jewelry stores
We're still looked at by some as sin-filled heathens
But we present ourselves in a negative manner, so we're giving them a reason
And I'm part of the problem, check out the gold I'm wearing
But I try to negate that aspect by the messages I'm sharing
I care about my people, but sometimes I feel like I'm part of a dying breed
And we've been warned about our demise, but we need to take heed
Well, I'm making it my personal responsibility to bring something different
So, I apologize for my demeanor, I'm just a little indignant
I'm tired of my people going through so much pain
Struggling so much, with so little to gain
Fame and fortune, yeah that may come
But what good is money if your community remains dumb
It's means nothing, that's why I can't allow that to happen
I'm trying to take my community to a place nobody could have imagined
The blaze of a revolution begins with a spark
I plan on being that blaze, I take that goal to heart

My goals and aspirations will not disappear, I can't even think about quitting

And the revolution may not be televised, but I'm gonna make sure it gets written

Love's a Trip

She told me I was taking her places she had never been before

She was afraid

Me, too

It was a trip I had never gone on before

The ticket said the final destination was love

Crazy thing is, I could have sworn I had been there with some other girl

But if I recall, that didn't work out very well

Was that the same love? Nah, it couldn't be

That love led me to someone who didn't seem to know the meaning of the word "truth"

"Sorry, I was upset, I think I may have torn up my ticket," I explained to the lady who was collecting them

Maybe, subconsciously I didn't want to go back

"Are you having second thoughts?"

I couldn't say yes because that would've hurt her and she didn't deserve that

"Nope, I'm just a little bit scared."

"I know. We both are, but I am here for you, just like you are here for me."

She held my hand as we moved passed the secured zone

I felt better

Yeah, this love had to be different than the last time

They said the flight was boarding

I gathered myself as we went aboard

I sat down quickly

The seatbelt light came on

I fastened mine because I had a feeling the flight would be filled with

many ups and downs

But this time I was ready

This time my trip was going to be a good one

Another deep breath was taken

Well.... here I go again

New Noose

Nowadays we got ropes, but they ain't hangin' from trees
I bought it from the store so it can hang off me
The diamonds from Sierra Leone are now in my home
Maybe that's why the gold diggin' women won't leave me alone
And yes, it's true, every kiss begins with k
But folks got sleighed for us to shine this way
It seems we don't actually care about the lost life of a man
As long as a few karats are dangling from your hands
And your bracelet comes courtesy of a new band of brothers
Those who became orphans when they all lost their mothers
Beauty on the outside hides the ugliness of its soul
Maybe it's called ice 'cause its birth was so cold
Got kids fiendin' for it by the time they're 3 years old
If we could sell ourselves to shine, it'll be just another one sold
People wanna know how we stay so fly
I guess our coolness increases when another one dies

God is the DJ

I once saw a shirt that said "God is the DJ"
I agreed, but wondered why it seems the song "Hardship" is the only thing that seemed to have any chance of a replay
@ least that's how it is whenever I'm in the club
I always hear bangin' beats when I'm an outsider, but as soon as I enter, things seem to change
God usually takes the energetic, up-tempo song and scratches in some blues
Such is my life
Seemingly in a hurry to reach depression
"Excuse me! Can you play……"
I try to think of that song I love, but hardly ever get to hear
It's no use, though
God has a huge crowd around him, I don't think He can hear me because of the headphones He's wearing
So, it's no wonder he doesn't respond to any of my requests
Every once and a while, I attempt to make another request, but I get the same result
@ least, God makes me believe He's not taking my request
But right when I'm about to give up and leave……
I hear my song begin to play

I smile as those who are unfamiliar with the music seem to clear the path for me

Not liking all of the attention, I'm hesitant for a moment, even though I had been waiting

"Do you wanna dance?" A young lady asks

She takes my hand and pulls me to the center

God smiles and points @ me just to acknowledge He had actually noticed me

I nodded my head and pointed back to say "Thank you."

Onlookers watched as I made a fool of myself

But the young lady I was dancing with gave me so much confidence I didn't even care

Time passed as it always does

My song ended

It was now time for someone else's request to be played

Still holding my new friend's hand, I realized something

The club is never about the individual who is dancing

It's always about the collective experience

We all know the party starts and ends with the DJ

So, our experience in life is similar to the one we often have in the club

We may not hear the song we requested @ the exact moment we request it

But we need to learn God is the DJ, and can't nobody rock a party like Him

The Store

Yeah I'm guilty, I'm a customer too
I find myself shopping in the store of you
A few minutes of your time is probably all I can afford
Forgive me for staring, but I can't look past the people I adore
You probably think I'm just feeding you a line
And you can't cry over spilled milk, so forgive me if I've wasted your time
They say this is the line for ten items or less
But your beauty gives me more than ten things I would like to express
I like your smile, I like your hair, I even like your stance
I like the fact we're still talking, and that you're giving me a chance
I like your personality and the way you move
If you'd be with me, then I'll like the way you choose
I like your southern accent and your zest for life
I like the fact you're not wearing a ring because you're not yet my wife
I like how you're not into people because of their money
And even when they're corny, you act like my jokes are hysterically funny
I like how you have that sparkle in your eyes
And how my sentimental statements of truth have you ready to cry
Those are just the things I could come up with off of the top of my head
I'm sure if I thought a little more, I would have come up with other things instead

But I've said too much about the things you probably already know
I was just wondering, when it comes to love, are you opened or closed?

To Mom

To show my appreciation, I would have to speak for the rest of my life
I thank you for the advice you gave when things weren't going right
Your love is contagious and so is your smile
When I'm around you, I feel the same safety I did when I was a child
But we live in different states, so I don't see you everyday
But no amount of distance can take away the fact that my mom is great
Without your guidance, some of my turbulence… I wouldn't have made it through
That's why emotionally, I can't help but look up to you
Because of you and Dad, people say I turned out to be a good person
Ya'll taught that if I haven't reached my goals… well, I need to keep workin'
I'm lurking near and dear to success
And until ya'll can retire, then I can't rest
All of these words are not just fiction, I promise they're fact
I'll continue to show my love and gratitude everyday, I don't need a holiday for that

My Life's Symphony

The conductor of my life's symphony takes the stage
Anticipation and silence fill the room in preparation for the symphony's start
Tick, tick
The conductor lets us know things are about to begin without saying a word
The opus starts off fast, energetic, and on a bit of a jovial note
That soon changes
The pace slows down and there now is a very somber mood
Pause
The silence is now deafening
Now the violinists are instructed to play a longer combination of 'sad' music
But there is no response, at least not for a while
The intensity increases with every anticipated bow stroke
Still……nothing
Emotions from the participants intensify, just as life does
There is no controlling life, nor the emotions that come along with it
The conductor has now lost control of the music
Just like I sometimes feel I have lost control of my life
Both try to regain control, but the difficulty is increasingly difficult

The onlookers of my orchestra shake their heads collectively as the musicians try to get back on track
Acting is if they have never stumbled
Yeah, that's a lie!
The once staccato notes ringing out form the brass section have now slurred into the unrecognizable
Some would call the moment disgusting
Some would call it necessary chaos; needed to keep the symphony going
Others just called it real
The chaos continues for a while before it, too has stopped
I guess nothing lasts forever
Now it seems everyone playing the music is waiting to see how things are going to turn out, just as the audience is
They have reached the point of the symphony that is left for improvisation
This, like everyone's experiences are always different
It means different things to different people
What one person sees as negative, another may see as a chance to do better
I don't know how I see things, though
My vision is blurry and sometimes I have to close my eyes and just let the symphony happen
Sometimes, we feel we have to force certain things to occur, but when we do that, the outcome generally isn't what we were looking for
So, as much as I want to, I try not to force anything

Again, I just have to sit back and let the music happen

Regardless of how it turns out, this is my symphony

And to me, it's a masterpiece

New Era

They do it with simplistic designs

I'm more about simplistic rhymes

But both are still over some folks' heads

They show support of a team, I'm all about supporting the dream, but both showcase what others may dread

They display different colors, different letters, and different teams

I tell about my different views and difference of opinions, so I guess they are just as different as me

Each one purchased has a very unique story to tell

Each one of poems do too, so I guess we have that in common, as well

Some wear their new eras backwards, I guess it's just their style

I write down words, but we both create things we hope are able to make folks smile

I guess I have gravitated towards them because their company is called New Era, and that's exactly where I'm trying to lead

So, if it takes the purchasing of products to be inspired, then I most certainly must proceed

I'm trying to get right like the side I tilt my hat to once it has been placed upon my head

I pray my actions will confirm anything else I have ever done, written, and or said

Some may find it dumb for me to write about an item, especially something like a hat

I say it's ironic because I'm telling you my potential can't be 'capped'

On my hats, I normally have a T, standing for Texas; some say it may be for talented, but also always bringing the truth

Now I've said what represents me, how about telling me what represents you?

My Reality

I constantly find myself alone

Nobody here with me, nobody available on the phone

Maybe in a former life, I was constantly a jerk

Maybe that's the reason I always get hurt

I still try to do for others like I wish others would

I know that won't always be reciprocated, even though it should

My karma's my armor, positivity's my shield

I continue to live my life and I refuse to yield

Maybe that's the reason I'm hated so much

And perhaps that's the reason my life is so tough

Contrary to what is believed, I don't think I would have it any other way

Because my downfalls and failures have made me what I am today

My reality would probably have other people stressed

But even in the midst of my shortcomings, I consider myself blessed

Let Love Lie

Too many times I hear people saying, "We need to let love lie."
But if love lives in lies, it'll most certainly die
And if I tried, I still couldn't tell you why
Many would rather hide behind loneliness because they're always in the shadow of their pride
People cheat on their better judgment because of affairs of the heart
Forget Cupid's arrows because the words blazing from our mouths are killing him before he starts
So, there are no little love helpers in red
Feeding romantic visions into our heads
Forget the positivity others have said
Not knowing it's our own fault love is dead
Several times I have tried to force my blindness on things others found painfully easy to see
More times than not, I would not question her, but always question me
At times, love makes a fool of us all
It seems my romantic opportunities never are knocking, so that's why I keep giving them a call
Sometimes they answer, sometimes they don't
Sometimes they want to move forward, other times they won't
I admit, there are many times when this particular emotion has me baffled
And though I'm lost, I am constantly willing to go through the hassle

Willing to try and find hope to get on the path

Only to be hurt again and have my hope dashed

But I know my negative moments most certainly won't last

I try to think more about my future, instead of dwelling on my past

These thoughts are the truth, not allowing love to lie

And if I live in hopes of love, then love can't die

Alien Nation

I know technically I'm a stranger if you don't know my name
But just because you don't know how to refer to me doesn't mean you have to look at me like I'm strange
I find it crazy when I say, "Hello." to someone and they act as if I didn't speak
Or seeing that my color alone is enough to make someone cross to the other side of the street
Yes, I'm Black, and they may be white
But it doesn't mean all of my actions are wrong, just like it doesn't mean all of theirs are right
We're all different; whether it be because of gender, race or creed
But if I don't judge you, please make sure you don't judge me
It's sad how many of us treat others as if they're from other planets
And if they walk into a room, we act as though we can't stand it
We point while snobbishly putting our noses in the air
While waving off interactions like we just don't care
Acting like we're better than others, when in reality we're scared
Living a life of separation is something you actually can't bear
But no more soapbox, I'll return you to your regularly scheduled station
I guess we'll keep living our lives separated, in the days of the alien nation

Photographic Memory

Some say I have a photographic memory and I believe it's true
Because I'm able to imagine the perfect picture of you whenever I feel blue
I sense your scent even when you're not around
And even when reliving our arguments, it is next to impossible for me to frown
Don't get me wrong, our relationship is not perfect, but that's where we're headed
And the time we're apart, every second is the one that's dreaded
But I know you love me, you tell me 365 days a year
Me − you, well that = one of my biggest fears
Our love is like the one described by my friend when he talks about his relationship with his wife
I mocked him at first, but I see that love = life
My heart beats as yours does, I breathe with the power of your lungs
We were born worlds apart, but are constantly moving closer to becoming one
I love you more than I have ever loved anyone else
And my bank account could be permanently fixated @ 0, but as long as I have you, I have infinite wealth
And this ain't no, " I'm writing this poem so I can get a girl" type stuff

This is to everyone acting too gangster for love, consider this a poem calling your bluff

Because there is not a person alive who wishes to be alone

And if you say you do, here's your crown because stupidity is obviously your throne

Well, I'm only single 'cause I'm too scared to mingle, but that's on me

I love the thought of love and I know one day she'll love me

When it comes to my thoughts, you are my first, and many times my last

You are my future, that's why I can disregard my past

You are the greatest love I've never had

The reason why even when I'm happy, part of me still remains sad

Some say I have a photographic memory, but maybe it's a little tainted

Perhaps that's why I'm able to imagine the picture of perfection… even before it's painted

My Walkman

Back in the day, my grandmother bought me a Walkman

I had to be around ten and back then, none of my friends had a way to carry around their music

But Big Mama made sure I was different

Even @ that young age, music equaled happiness

So, she made it possible to take my joy wherever I went

I could remember anticipating my school day to be over so I could enjoy my music

"Oooh, is that a Walkman?" They would ask

"Yep! My Big Mama bought it for me!"

"You're lucky!"

I already knew that, though. It just took a music player for them to see

My family, on the other hand, knew what I knew

"What's in the walkman today, Jake?"

I called out the name of what I was listening to

No matter what it was, they would always smile

I guess music always had that affect on people

But who knows if we would have shared those moments if it weren't for Big Mama

Somehow, she always found a way to make everyone happy

That's part of the reason I loved that Walkman so much

It meant something to me

It symbolized Big Mama's love

It seemed to have memories & smiles built in with its other features

It brought back times when one relative would ask the younger one a question about music and it would bring them a little bit closer

The Walkman

The sad thing is, over time, the Walkman and the happiness that came along with it were lost

No more family joy

No more hangin' out with each other

Worst of all….no more Big Mama

So everything that the music player symbolized was gone

Sure, over the years I got other music players

Yeah, technology improved in just about every aspect

But nothing has been able to come close to that overall feeling I got from my Walkman

Today, I'm able to take tons of music with me wherever I go

In that regard, life is good

But to be honest, I would give it all up just to have my Walkman back

(Untitled)

When it comes to my words, I can't always say them vocally
Get apprehensive about my thoughts, so I put them in the form of poetry
Gettin' butterflies like M. Jackson and Floetry
When I even think about trying to get you to go with me
To the happiest place that exists on earth
Not talkin' Disneyland, it's where I'm your man, and you see your worth
A place where the price of platinum plummets each time you smile
And you have the years of inner peace you haven't felt in a while
But maybe my aspirations are a bit far fetched
And maybe I have unrealistic expectations, that's why I'm not in a relationship yet
Maybe I have yet to find someone who cares
And at times we all see that life is not fair
But if you dare to continue reaching higher
Maybe the love you find will be better than what you think you desire
But don't be like me, whatever's on your heart, force your mouth to say
Only then will love not be a four-letter word as you live a life full of Valentine's Days

Another Girl Lost

She was a beautiful girl, but had low self-esteem
Everyday she woke up, someone treated her mean
If it wasn't her father, it was someone @ school
She had untapped potential, but was treated like a fool
Her eyes were the windows to a tormented soul
She had a warm heart, but her world was cold
She asked several people for help, but she was always denied
Loneliness was killing her & every night she cried
She couldn't understand why she had to be hurt
And why nobody ever told her she had any worth
So one day she got tired, but didn't know what to do
Couldn't find an answer until she bought a .22
A few hundred dollars was all it cost
I guess we all fronted the bill for another girl lost

Waiting

In high school, I used to put my books in the locker
Just to get a glimpse of the embodiment of beauty while feeling like a stalker
"Hey Jacob." Yep, every once and again she would speak
Her words were like asthma, taking the breath out of me
I'd eventually take a deep breath and I tried to reply
But alas it was too late, I saw her leaving out of the corner of my eye
She was too fly, at least that's how I felt
So, I ended up alone because I didn't have confidence in self
That's probably what I deserved for being so shy
Perhaps that's why there was no we, only I
And I tried, @ least in my brain, I did
The age of a man, but feeling more like a kid
Looking back, I realize now, I had problems
But years later, I have yet to become smart enough to solve them
Yeah, I still find myself tripping and then falling in love
But the women don't reply, so I end up pulling myself up
Maybe one day a lady will actually enjoy one of my lines
And I won't have to fall back to the therapy of my pen, pad, and rhymes
They say if you let something go and it comes back, then it is truly yours
Well, I let go of my emotions a while ago and waiting on love to be returned is a daunting chore

Hopefully when it returns, it will be in the hands of that one special lady

Until then, I guess I have no choice but to sit here.... waiting

?

I don't know if my glass is half-full, or if it's half-empty
If I should continue chasing dreams, or if my goals are unreachable and there just to tempt me
I can't determine if I'm a glutton for pain, or anorexic when it comes to pleasure
If I'm at all an intellectual, or just idiotically clever
If I'm just rushing through the good times, or moving too slow to prosper
Reading between lines that don't exist, or not seeing what the world has to offer
Trying to use every second as if it's my last
Or wasting all of my time as if I can get it back
Sometimes some can't tell if I have a halo on my head or if I have horns
I don't know if folks will enjoy my death because they despise the day I was born
I wish I could tell if I could be easy to remember or hard to forget
If my viewpoint of life has been correct of if it should have been the opposite
I don't know if I'll be a role model or inspire others on what not to be
I have no idea if we will continue to be captivated by mediocrity or if extraordinary will finally set us free
Who knows if I will be well off with some sort of notoriety

Or if I will be just another meaningless number, just a small part of a large society
I wish I knew if my life would be more abstract, or closer to something painted by the numbers
If the days of my life were alarmingly vibrant or gray enough for others to slumber
The things I don't know now, I pray I find out later
And those things I do learn, I hope they make future generations greater
For if my life is lived with honor as I try to avoid disgrace
Then all of my questions will be answered as I leave the world a better place

(Untitled)

The powers that be won't allow me to break free
Which may lead to the death of me, almost inevitably
Shackles of inequity seem to be my destiny
Keeping me connected to those who won't let me be
Those whose objective is to keep me from maximizing my potential
Stressing my mental while their method of disrespect remain mostly subliminal
Which is far more dangerous than those methods I can easily see
Searching for answers on why people continue hating on me
But maybe this isn't the time for me to concoct my own answer
Maybe I should let the unknown fester and grow like a psychological cancer
And let my problems get to a point where they overthrow my brain
Changing life's priorities and in turn bypassing joy while seemingly searching for pain
But really, I'm just searching for change
Trying to leave behind the vehicles of the things trying to drive me insane
Certainly that seems to be on the road less traveled
Seeing so many followers in the world leaves me baffled
I'm dumbfounded @ how many I have found to be dumb
No longer being able to feel their pain because I have become numb
I'd run from the madness, but I seem to be frozen

Not allowed to fix what the things others can't even see is broken
Like I said before, I'm still choking on my insecurities and obsessions
But no longer in denial while using my paper to release my confessions
Life sometimes teaches lessons that I have no desire to learn
I heard "it gets greater later," so I'm just waiting my turn
I guess I shouldn't let the uncontrollable leave me stressed
I should calm down while not allowing anyone to impede my progress
But I suspect I get upset about past, present, and future actions I regret
I fret about things others seemingly choose to neglect
But it's not just me because other people's actions are suspect, so I'll convict them of the crime
They'll be sentenced (out of my) life because they're trying to stealing my peace of mind
And I know I shouldn't hold grudges because they say time heals all wounds
I heard happiness is a buffet, so I'd like my chance to consume
In the end, I guess my struggles have made me who I am
I'll keep battling through it all, just so I'll be proud of myself for doing the best that I can

In Remembrance of Grandpa

We said we had prepared for his death, but in all honesty, we were lying
We may have show faces of stone externally, but internally, we were crying
Tears were streaming inside as if they are trying to wash away the pain
The death of William Jacobs, Sr. means our lives will never be the same
He may have not been the tallest, but his impact was huge
Giants would be dwarfed by his legacy and nobody can ever fill his shoes
Just trying to be like him would be an impossible task
And although we know death is certain, we still wish we could have him back
But certain wishes are unrealistic, for we all have our place, we all have our time
And although he is gone physically, he will never leave our minds
Years ago, God called his wife back, leaving him alone
Now, there will be no more loneliness for their spirits because he too, is going home
Grandpa, now you'll be reunited with Big Mama, and it'll be just like you remember
And we'll see you both again once the calendar of our lives have reached its December

The One

They say nice guys finish last, but I continue to pursue
I see others moving fast, so what am I gonna do?
I hear some people say what I want, they've already had
So as I deal with my tribulations, they do nothing but laugh
It's to be expected because it's a dog-eat-dog world
And if it's like that for all other aspects, why would it be any different when it comes to girls?
It can't, and I know my environment may never change
And though she has been other people's goal, our reasons for going after her weren't the same
She can be mean, she can be nice, and there are so many reasons why she's the one people seek
Her attitudes could make you want to yell, but I'll shut up just to hear her speak
In my eyes, she is one of the best things God has ever created
So when other dudes see her with me, I can understand the hatred
I don't visualize her past because really, there is no need
We are together for the here and now, and I can't wait to proceed

My World, My Words

From the day I was born, to when I first learned to speak
I knew I had words of importance buried deep within me
With everything I write, to everything I say
If it's going to be expressed, it'll be done my way
Regardless of the consequences, I'm going to speak my mind
If I'm verbally isolated, then so be it, fine
I've never been one to go along with the crowd
Simply because popularity is not all that I'm about
If something needs to be stated, I'm not going to be politically correct
'Cause I don't write for your approval, nor to get you upset
But if either action occurs, then I guess it's deserved
And it's only absurd if someone alters my words
Supposedly a picture equals a thousand words written
Then I suppose my prose is providing a different vision
One that if a blind man closed his eyes he could see
The word-filled portrait that was painted by me
And if you flip the pages fast enough, my story will start to move like animation
My time of focus and concentration will then lead to your fascination
Artists say, "How can his words be so vivid, so bright?
It's like he applies what I do with a brush to the way he writes."
As if I write and type in braille, I'm trying to give you words you can feel

I can't comprehend fake, so all I do is keep it real
My world was placed upon me, it wasn't something I could choose
My words are therapeutic, the cure for my blues
If you put my world with my words, what I hope you will find
Is both entertaining and enlightening, for they are the confessions of my cluttered mind

Thank You

It may be unusual to have a thank you section to close out a collection of poetry, but I don't always follow the path of normality. With that being said, I would first like to thank God. I know it is because of you I was even able to write this book. I know these words cannot come from me alone.

To my parents, Janice and Gregory, Sr. , I thank you for raising me to be the man I am. I want you to know I am forever grateful and there is no amount of money, nor words, that can ever repay you for that. To my little brother Greg (II), I thank you for inspiring me to keep moving forward. Little brother, you have helped me out more than you will ever know. I hope I can make you proud.

To my cousins, aunts, uncles, and everybody else, I appreciate ya'll. I'm glad to see there are members of my family who are still the same people I grew up with. Your support and encouragement means more than you know. Thank you.

Throughout my life, I have also been blessed to be around many people who I now consider to be a part of my extended family (and please believe my parents know about the vast majority of ya'll). Eddie, I've known you since I was 12 years old and I just appreciate you for remaining the same person and friend throughout the years. I know you've got my back, even though we don't speak as often as we used to.

Daniel and Equasta, I thank the two of you for lending me an ear whenever I needed it. I also appreciate how you two are able to make sure God is a part of the conversation to help me out through some of life's trials and tribulations. Dominique, what can I say about you, little sister? Your spirit is uplifting. I'm glad you're around and I hope you make sure you stay around.

Chandra, we may not be biologically related, but you are my big sister. You have had my back since the first day we met and things have never changed. Words can't express my appreciation. O'Bryan, when I just felt like runnin' off at the mouth with some stupid stuff, I appreciate you allowing me to do so. Please believe the song "Heavy Duty Tub Mats" is on the way (inside joke).

Tommy, if it weren't for you, I think that transition from Texas to Florida would've been much more difficult. Thank you. Roy, another person I've known since I was in junior high school. You were crazy then and you're crazy now… make sure you stay that way, homie! Dottie, I know we just recently got back in contact with each other, but don't think I will ever forget how you and Chandra looked out for me. Your little brother, with the nickname that won't be mentioned here, has your back like I know you have mine.

Angie, I mean Angela Jackson. Who would've thought that girl who was in the orchestra at O.W. Holmes would be one of my closest friends? Thanks for stayin' around. If all of that wasn't enough, after I left

Dallas, I was blessed with so many more family members in Tallahassee, Fl.

PJ, aka 'Bles,' you were one of the first people Tommy and I met at FAMU. The very first time you saw ask, you asked us for directions like we knew where we were going. As you may remember, we had no idea. I guess God was saying all three of us would need each other in order to find our way.

Then, we have the boys known as 212 or The 'Partment (don't ask). Skyler, Karl and Byron. Ya'll are family for real. Ya'll are the people who always allowed me to be me no matter how goofy, dorky, or childish I was. Thank you. I pray that each one of you is able to reach the level of success you deserve.

Brandon aka B Major, I appreciate you being there as a supporter of my music, and of me in general. Hopefully you can say the same about me. Adarryl, there were times I've wanted to give up on a lot of things, but you have helped me keep going. The #1 Haitian, aka Jim, all I can say is… thanks for being you, homie! Wayne, simply you have a personality like no other, but that's partially why we get along.

John aka J5, you've been a supporter of my writing as far back as I could remember. You always kept it real and I know you will continue to do so. Debraca, when we first met, I thought you were a stuck-up person that I didn't really want to know. I am certainly glad I was sooooo wrong about you. I now know you are one of the people I can truly count on.

Ta'veka, like J5, you truly keep it real. Also, you've made sure a lot of the team had the mental strength to keep going while we were at work. Who knows where I would've been without you and those Waffle House trips? Jewels, I appreciate you and your militant ways. Believe it or not, the world really needs more people like you.

Jennifer, although recently you've been somewhat m.i.a., you've been very vital in me trying to pursue my dreams. I hope you are still going after yours. Lyndsey, so much could be said, but I'm not gonna put it all out there. I will say that I thank you for showing an interest in the things that were of interest to me. That really means a lot.

Nicole aka Maria (another inside joke), thanks for being there through some of those difficult times. I appreciate it and value your friendship. To John A., the future is yours, man! Thanks for showing me we all can do things of importance. Obama was just the start, I already know.

Melba aka Melbaton, (yet another inside joke), you gave me the notebook and pens that started this whole project, so I thank you . Not to mention the fact that you've really been a good friend to me. Thanks for everything.

Miranda, I thank you for helping me find my way when I was almost lost. If there is anything you or Amber need, you know I got you. Oh and Amber, remember that I said you need to stay focused on school, and not any of those other things. Ketrina, Fred, and little Fred, thank you for being yourselves. You have shown that you cared about me pressing on even when it seemed like I didn't even care. Thanks.

Thank you to AB. You certainly have put up with a lot from me. I appreciate it. Not many women can deal with my stubbornness, so I appreciate the effort. I needed all of the help I could get, and you certainly did your part.

To any women who I've been in a relationship with, or even tried to be in one with, I thank you, too. I will never publicly say anything negative about you. For whatever reason things didn't work out, but it's all good. Please know the poems about heartache or love may have been inspired by you, so if nothing else, I thank you for the inspiration to create.

I am absolutely certain I have forgotten a ton of people. I apologize for that. Your omission was not on purpose, trust me. Please blame my mind and definitely not my heart. Look for your recognition in the next book!

Last, but not least, I would like to thank the readers. I thank you for supporting a person with a dream. I pray the words of this book don't disappoint you, but if they do, know that I am human. I am always trying to grow and I promise you won't see me stop marching towards progress!

I truly thank you all!

Jacob G. Grovey

www.ingramcontent.com/pod-product-compliance
Ingram Content Group UK Ltd.
Pitfield, Milton Keynes, MK11 3LW, UK
UKHW022225230426
12048UKWH00016BA/1064